P9-DMD-357

OTTAWA PUBLIC LIBRARY
BIBLIOTHEQUE PUBLIQUE D'OTTAWA.

ZOOM In on Animals!

African Elephants
Up Close

Carmen Bredeson

Enslow Elementary

CONTENTS

WORDS TO KNOW

female—A girl animal or person.

grasslands—Land where most plants are grasses.

herd—A family group of elephants.

male—A boy animal or person.

wrinkles (RIHN kulhz)—Deep lines in the skin.

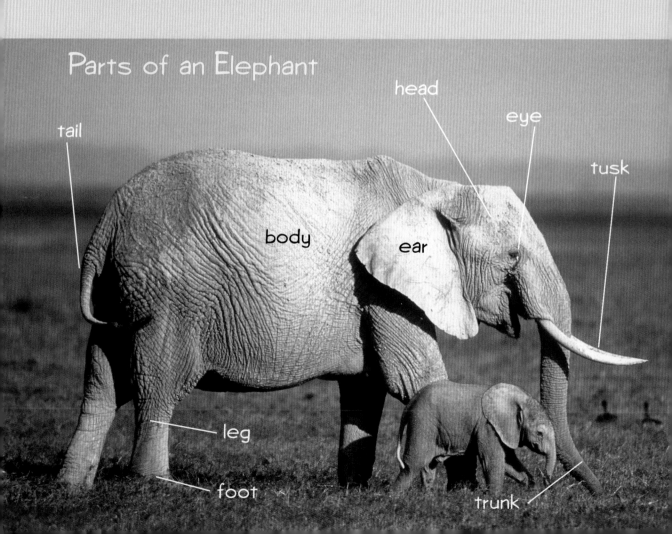

Parts of an Elephant

tail

head

eye

tusk

body

ear

leg

foot

trunk

AFRICAN ELEPHANT

African elephants are the biggest
land animals. They can live to be
50 years old.

ELEPHANT EARS

African elephants live in hot, dry grasslands.
They keep cool by flapping their huge ears.
When an elephant is scared or angry, it sticks its
ears out.

ELEPHANT SKIN

UP CLOSE

Elephant skin is gray. It has many wrinkles and bumps. Even elephant skin can get a sunburn, so elephants roll in the mud. The mud covers the skin so it does not burn. The mud keeps the bugs away, too!

ELEPHANT TRUNKS

UP CLOSE

An elephant's trunk is a handy tool. It is used for smelling, drinking, and making loud noises. It can pick up huge branches or little flowers to eat.

A trunk can also spray water over an elephant's hot skin, or into its thirsty mouth.

ELEPHANT FOOD

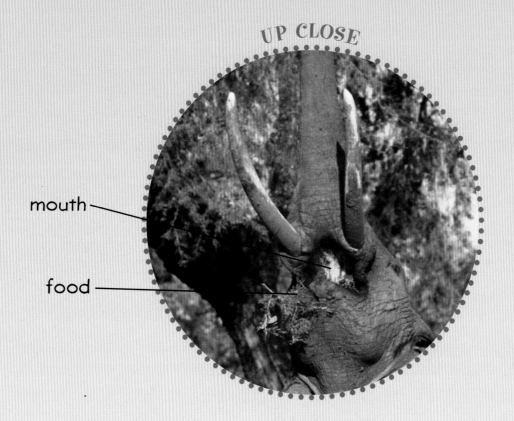

UP CLOSE

mouth

food

It takes a LOT of food to fill up an elephant. Elephants eat grass and flowers. They also eat tree bark, roots, and fruit. Chewing so much food takes a long time.

ELEPHANT TUSKS

UP CLOSE

An elephant's tusks are actually long, curved teeth. Tusks are used to dig up roots to eat. Sometimes elephants fight each other with their tusks.

ELEPHANT EYES

UP CLOSE

Mother elephants and their babies make up
a herd. The oldest female is the leader. She
watches with her eyes for danger. She leads
the herd to food and water.

ELEPHANT FEET

UP CLOSE

Males leave the herd when they are 12 to 14 years old. They live alone or in small groups.

In the spring, they walk for miles on their big, flat feet. They return to the herd to make new babies.

19

BABY ELEPHANTS

UP CLOSE

A mother elephant carries her growing baby in her body for two YEARS! Baby elephants weigh 200 to 300 pounds at birth.

Other elephants hug the baby with their trunks. They smell the little elephant to get to know it.

LIFE CYCLE

BABY
It weighs 200 to 300 pounds

YOUNG ADULT
It takes 12 to 14 years to grow up.

ADULT
It lives about 50 years.

22

LEARN MORE

Books

Eckart, Edana. *African Elephant*. New York: Children's Press, 2003.

Hall, Margaret. *Elephants and Their Calves*. Mankato, Minn.: Capstone Press, 2004.

Kulling, Monica. *Elephants: Life in the Wild*. New York: Random House Books for Young Readers, 2000.

Swanson, Diane. *Elephants*. Milwaukee: Gareth Stevens, 2004.

Web Sites

San Diego Zoo. *Elephants*.
<http://www.sandiegozoo.org/animalbytes/t-elephant.html>

Nature: The Elephants of Africa.
<http://www.pbs.org/wnet/nature/elephants/life.html>

INDEX

Series Literacy Consultant:
Allan A. De Fina, Ph.D.
Past President of the New Jersey Reading Association
Professor, Department of Literacy Education
New Jersey City University
Jersey City, New Jersey

Science Consultant:
Larry Killmar, Ph.D.
Deputy Director of Collections
San Diego Zoo
San Diego, California

Note to Parents and Teachers: The Zoom In on Animals! series supports the National Science Education Standards for K–4 science. The Words to Know section introduces subject-specific vocabulary words, including pronunciation and definitions. Early readers may need help with these new words.

For Andrew and Charlie, our wonderful grandsons

Enslow Elementary, an imprint of Enslow Publishers, Inc.

Enslow Elementary® is a registered trademark of Enslow Publishers, Inc.

Copyright © 2006 by Carmen Bredeson

All rights reserved.

No part of this book may be reproduced by any means without the written permission of the publisher.

Library of Congress Cataloging-in-Publication Data

Bredeson, Carmen.
African elephants up close / Carmen Bredeson.
  p. cm. — (Zoom in on animals!)
Includes bibliographical references and index.
ISBN 0-7660-2499-7 (hardcover)
1. African elephant—Juvenile literature. I. Title. II. Series.
QL737.P98B74 2006
599.67'4—dc22

2005003328

Printed in the United States

10 9 8 7 6 5 4 3 2 1

To Our Readers: We have done our best to make sure all Internet Addresses in this book were active and appropriate when we went to press. However, the author and the publisher have no control over and assume no liability for the material available on those Internet sites or on other Web sites they may link to. Any comments or suggestions can be sent by e-mail to comments@enslow.com or to the address on the back cover.

Photo Credits: Michael Nichols/National Geographic Image Collection, pp. 1, 6; © Juergen & Christine Sohns / Animals Animals, p. 3; © Peter Lillie / OSF / Animals Animals, pp. 4–5, 21; Nicole Duplaix /National Geographic Image Collection, p. 7; Bobby Model /National Geographic Image Collection, p. 8; © 2002–2004 Art Today, Inc., p. 9; Gerald Hinde/ABPL / Animals Animals, p. 10; Roy Toft /National Geographic Image Collection, p. 11; © D. Allen Photography / Animals Animals, p. 12; © McDonald Wildlife Photography / Animals Animals, pp. 13, 18; © M. Colbeck / OSF / Animals Animals, pp. 14, 22 (baby); Tim Davis / Photo Researchers, Inc., p. 15; Martin Harvey / Photo Researchers, Inc., p. 16; © Dr. Don W. Fawcett / Visuals Unlimited, p. 17; © M. Hamblin / OSF / Animals Animals, p. 19; © Manoj Shah / Animals Animals, p. 20.

Cover Photos: Michael Nichols/National Geographic Image Collection (large image); Martin Harvey/Photo Researchers, Inc. (eye); Bobby Model /National Geographic Image Collection (skin); McDonald Wildlife Photography / Animals Animals (foot).

Enslow Elementary
an imprint of
Enslow Publishers, Inc.
40 Industrial Road   PO Box 38
Box 398   Aldershot
Berkeley Heights, NJ 07922   Hants GU12 6BP
USA   UK
http://www.enslow.com

P9-DMD-356

Poems of the Countryside

PICTURES BY GORDON BENINGFIELD

This edition published by Selectabook,
Folly Road, Roundway, Devizes, Wiltshire SN10 2HR

Produced by TAJ Books,
Ferndown Gardens, Cobham, Surrey, KT11 2BH
www.tajbooks.com

First published 1987

Copyright © the Estate of Gordon Beningfield (pictures) and
Cameron Books (design and this selection of poetry)

All rights reserved. Without limiting the rights under copyright reserved above,
no part of this publication may be reproduced, stored in or introduced into a
retrieval system, or transmitted, in any form or by any means (electronic,
mechanical, photocopying, recording or otherwise), without the prior written
permission of both the copyright owner and the above publisher of this book

Selected and designed by Jill Hollis and Ian Cameron

Fcameron Books, PO Box 1, Moffat, DG10 9SU, UK
         www.cameronbooks.co.uk

British Library Cataloguing in Publication Data available

ISBN 0–670–81755–4

The following poems have been reprinted by permission of the publishers:
'Harvest Hymn' by John Betjeman, John Murray (Publishers) Ltd; 'Blackberry
Picking' by Seamus Heaney and 'Chalk Blue' by Stephen Spender, Faber & Faber
Ltd; 'the Future of Forestry' by C.S. Lewis, William Collins Sons & Co. Ltd;
'Falling Leaves' and 'Vegetation' by Kathleen Raine, Unwin Hyman; 'Snow Drop'
by Jon Silkin, Routledge & Kegan Paul; 'Man and Cows' by Andrew Young,
Martin Secker & Warburg Ltd. We thank Robert Gittings for his permission to
reprint 'The Fairy Tale'.

Pictures

Poems

Home-Thoughts, from Abroad

Oh, to be in England
Now that April's there,
And whoever wakes in England
Sees, some morning, unaware,
That the lowest boughs and the brushwood sheaf
Round the elm-tree bole are in tiny leaf,
While the chaffinch sings on the orchard bough
In England – now!

And after April, when May follows,
And the whitethroat builds, and all the swallows!
Hark, where my blossomed pear-tree in the hedge
Leans to the field and scatters on the clover
Blossoms and dewdrops – at the bent spray's edge –
That's the wise thrush; he sings each song twice over,
Lest you should think he never could recapture
The first fine careless rapture!
And though the fields look rough with hoary dew,
All will be gay when noontide wakes anew
The buttercups, the little children's dower
– Far brighter than this gaudy melon-flower!

ROBERT BROWNING (1812-89)

To One Who Has Been Long in City Pent

To one who has been long in city pent,
'Tis very sweet to look into the fair
And open face of heaven, – to breathe a prayer
Full in the smile of the blue firmament.
Who is more happy, when, with heart's content,
Fatigued he sinks into some pleasant lair
Of wavy grass, and reads a debonair
And gentle tale of love and languishment?
Returning home at evening, with an ear
Catching the notes of Philomel, – an eye
Watching the sailing cloudlet's bright career,
He mourns that day so soon has glided by:
E'en like the passage of an angel's tear
That falls through the clear ether silently.

JOHN KEATS (1795-1821)

The Glory

The glory of the beauty of the morning, –
The cuckoo crying over the untouched dew;
The blackbird that has found it, and the dove
That tempts me on to something sweeter than love;
White clouds ranged even and fair as new-mown hay;
The heat, the stir, the sublime vacancy
Of sky and meadow and forest and my own heart:-
The glory invites me, yet it leaves me scorning
All I can ever do, all I can be,
Beside the lovely of motion, shape, and hue,
The happiness I fancy fit to dwell
In beauty's presence. Shall I now this day
Begin to seek as far as heaven, as hell,
Wisdom or strength to match this beauty, start
And tread the pale dust pitted with small dark drops,
In hope to find whatever it is I seek,
Hearkening to short-lived happy-seeming things
That we know naught of, in the hazel copse?
Or must I be content with discontent
As larks and swallows are perhaps with wings?
And shall I ask at the day's end once more
What beauty is, and what I can have meant
By happiness? And shall I let all go,
Glad, weary, or both? Or shall I perhaps know
That I was happy oft and oft before,
Awhile forgetting how I am fast pent,
How dreary-swift, with naught to travel to,
Is Time? I cannot bite the day to the core.

EDWARD THOMAS (1878-1917)

To Nature

It may indeed be phantasy, when I
Essay to draw from all created things
Deep, heartfelt, inward joy that closely clings;
And trace in leaves and flowers that round me lie
Lessons of love and earnest piety.
So let it be; and if the wide world rings
In mock of this belief, it brings
Nor fear, nor grief, nor vain perplexity.
So will I build my altar in the fields,
And the blue sky my fretted dome shall be,
And the sweet fragrance that the wild flower yields
Shall be the incense I will yield to Thee,
Thee only God! and thou shalt not despise
Even me, the priest of this poor sacrifice.

SAMUEL TAYLOR COLERIDGE (1772-1834)

The succession of the foure sweet months

First, April, she with mellow showrs
Opens the way for early flowers;
Then after her comes smiling May,
In a more rich and sweet aray:
Next enters June, and brings us more
Jems, than those two, that went before:
Then (lastly) July comes, and she
More wealth brings in, than all those three.

ROBERT HERRICK (1591-1674)

Field Flowers

Ye field flowers! the gardens eclipse you, 'tis true,
Yet, wildings of Nature, I dote upon you,
For ye waft me to summers of old,
When the earth teem'd around me with fairy delight,
And when daisies and buttercups gladden'd my sight,
Like treasures of silver and gold.

I love you for lulling me back into dreams
Of the blue Highland mountains and echoing streams,
And of birchen glades breathing their balm,
While the deer was seen glancing in sunshine remote,
And the deep mellow crush of the wood-pigeon's note
Made music that sweeten'd the calm.

Not a pastoral song has a pleasanter tune
Than ye speak to my heart, little wildings of June:
Of old ruinous castles ye tell,
Where I thought it delightful your beauties to find,
When the magic of Nature first breathed on my mind,
And your blossoms were part of her spell.

Even now what affections the violet awakes!
What loved little islands, twice seen in their lakes,
Can the wild water-lily restore!
What landscapes I read in the primrose's looks,
And what pictures of pebbled and minnowy brooks,
In the vetches that tangled their shore.

Earth's cultureless buds, to my heart ye were dear.
Ere the fever of passion, or ague of fear,
Had scathed my existence's bloom;
Once I welcome you more, in life's passionless stage,
With the visions of youth to revisit my age,
And I wish you to grow on my tomb.

THOMAS CAMPBELL (1777-1844)

Chalk Blue

The Chalk Blue (clinging to
A harebell stem, its loop,
From which there hangs the flower
Shaken by the wind that shakes
The butterfly also) –
Opens now, now shuts, its wings,
Opening, closing, like a hinge,
Sprung at touch of sun or shadow.
   Open, the wings mirror
All the cloudless sky.
Shut, the milky underwing
Cloud-mirroring, is bordered by
Orange spots nailed there
By a pigmy hammering.

STEPHEN SPENDER (b 1909)

To Daisies, not to shut so soon

Shut not so soon; the dull-eyed night
Has not as yet begun
To make a seizure on the light,
Or to seal up the sun.

No marigolds yet closèd are,
No shadows great appear;
Nor doth the early shepherd's star
Shine like a spangle here.

Stay but till my Julia close
Her life-begetting eye,
And let the whole world then dispose
Itself to live or die.

ROBERT HERRICK (1591-1674)

Where the Bee Sucks

Where the bee sucks, there suck I:
In a cowslip's bell I lie;
There I couch when owls do cry.
On the bat's back I do fly
After summer merrily:
Merrily, merrily, shall I live now,
Under the blossom that hangs on the bough.

WILLIAM SHAKESPEARE (1564-1616)

from *Summer*

Welcome, ye shades! ye bowery thickets, hail!
Ye lofty pines! ye venerable oaks!
Ye ashes wild, resounding o'er the steep!
Delicious is your shelter to the soul,
As to the hunted hart the sallying spring,
Or stream full-flowing, that his swelling sides
Laves, as he floats along the herbaged brink.
Cool, through the nerves, your pleasing comfort glides;
The heart beats glad; the fresh expanded eye
And ear resume their watch; the sinews knit;
And life shoots swift through all the lighten'd limbs.

JAMES THOMSON (1834-82)

Man and Cows

I stood aside to let the cows
Swing past me with their wrinkled brows,
Bowing their heads as they went by
As to a woodland deity
To whom they turned mute eyes
To save them from the plaguing god of flies.

And I too cursed Beelzebub,
Watching them stop to rub
A bulging side or bony haunch
Against a trunk or pointing branch
And lift a tufted tail
To thresh the air with its soft flail.

They stumbled heavily down the slope,
As Hethor led them or the hope
Of the lush meadow-grass,
While I remained, thinking it was
Strange that we both were held divine,
In Egypt these, man once in Palestine.

ANDREW YOUNG (1885-1971)

A Contemplation upon Flowers

Brave flowers – that I could gallant it like you,
And be as little vain!
You come abroad, and make a harmless show,
And to your beds of earth again.
You are not proud: you know your birth:
For your embroider'd garments are from earth.

You do obey your months and times, but I
Would have it ever Spring:
My fate would know no Winter, never die,
Nor think of such a thing.
O that I could my bed of earth but view
And smile, and look as cheerfully as you!

O teach me to see Death and not to fear,
But rather to take truce!
How often have I seen you at a bier,
And there look fresh and spruce!
You fragrant flowers! then teach me, that my breath
Like yours may sweeten and perfume my death.

HENRY KING (1592-1669)

Foliage

Come forth, and let us through our hearts receive
The joy of verdure! – see, the honied lime
Showers cool green light o'er banks where wild-flowers weave
Thick tapestry; and woodbine tendrils climb
Up the brown oak from buds of moss and thyme.
The rich deep masses of the sycamore
Hang heavy with the fulness of their prime,
And the white poplar, from its foliage hoar,
Scatters forth gleams like moonlight, with each gale
That sweeps the boughs: – the chestnut flowers are past,
The crowning glories of the hawthorn fail,
But arches of sweet eglantine are cast
From every hedge: – Oh! never may we lose,
Dear friend! our fresh delight in simplest nature's hues!

FELICIA DOROTHEA HEMANS (1793-1835)

The Selfsame Song

A bird sings the selfsame song,
With never a fault in its flow,
That we listened to here those long
Long years ago.

A pleasing marvel is how
A strain of such rapturous rote
Should have gone on thus till now
Unchanged in a note!

– But it's not the selfsame bird. –
No: perished to dust is he …
As also are those who heard
That song with me.

THOMAS HARDY (1840-1928)

Self-Pity

I never saw a wild thing
sorry for itself.
A small bird will drop frozen dead from a bough
without ever having felt sorry for itself.

D.H. LAWRENCE (1885-1930)

A Living

A man should never earn his living,
if he earns his life he'll be lovely.

A bird
picks up its seeds or little snails
between heedless earth and heaven
in heedlessness.

But, the plucky little sport, it gives to life
song, and chirruping, gay feathers, fluff-shadowed warmth
and all the unspeakable charm of birds hopping
and fluttering and being birds.
– And we, we get it all from them for nothing.

D.H. LAWRENCE (1885-1930)

A Boy's Song

Where the pools are bright and deep,
Where the grey trout lies asleep,
Up the river and over the lea,
That's the way for Billy and me.

Where the blackbird sings the latest,
Where the hawthorn blooms the sweetest,
Where the nestlings chirp and flee,
That's the way for Billy and me.

Where the mowers mow the cleanest,
Where the hay lies thick and greenest,
There to track the homeward bee,
That's the way for Billy and me.

Where the hazel bank is steepest,
Where the shadow falls the deepest,
Where the clustering nuts fall free,
That's the way for Billy and me.

Why the boys should drive away
Little sweet maidens from the play,
Or love to banter and fight so well,
That's the thing I never could tell.

But this I know, I love to play
Through the meadow, among the hay;
Up the water and over the lea,
That's the way for Billy and me.

JAMES HOGG (1770-1835)

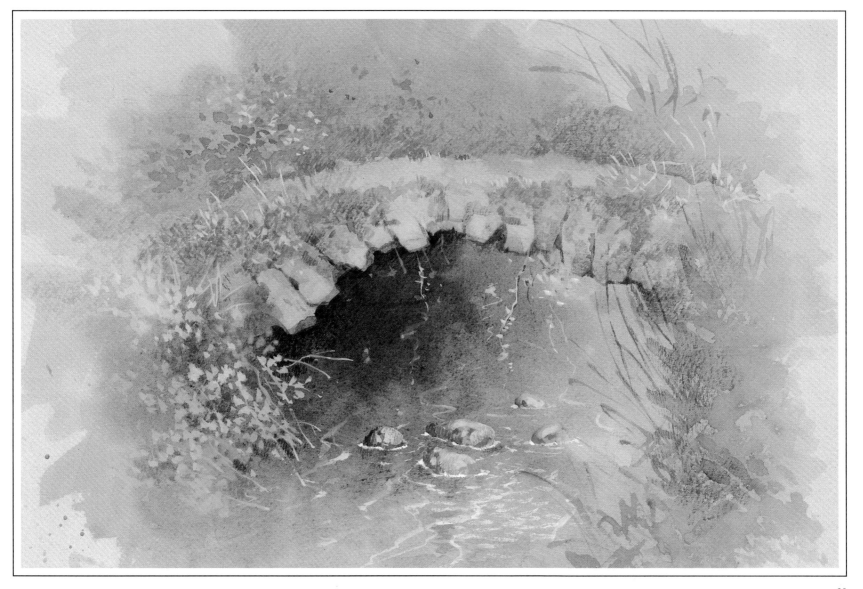

The Rainy Summer

There's much afoot in heaven and earth this year;
The winds hunt up the sun, hunt up the moon,
Trouble the dubious dawn, hasten the drear
Height of a threatening noon.

No breath of boughs, no breath of leaves, of fronds
May linger or grow warm; the trees are loud;
The forest, rooted, tosses in her bonds,
And strains against the cloud.

No scents may pause within the garden-fold;
The rifled flowers are cold as ocean-shells;
Bees, humming in the storm, carry their cold
Wild honey to cold cells.

ALICE MEYNELL (1847-1922)

from *Is Life Worth Living?*

Is life worth living? Yes, so long
As Spring revives the year,
And hails us with the cuckoo's song,
To show that she is here;
So long as May of April takes,
In smiles and tears, farewell,
And windflowers dapple all the brakes,
And primroses the dell;
While children in the woodlands yet
Adorn their little laps
With ladysmock and violets,
And daisy-chain their caps;
While over orchard daffodils
Cloud-shadows float and fleet,
And ouzel pipes and laverock trills,
And young lambs buck and bleat;
So long as that which bursts the bud
And swells and tunes the rill,
Makes springtime in the maiden's blood,
Life is worth living still.

ALFRED AUSTIN (1835-1913)

The Hill

Breathless, we flung us on the windy hill,
Laughed in the sun, and kissed the lovely grass.
You said, 'Through glory and ecstasy we pass;
Wind, sun, and earth remain, the birds sing still,
When we are old, are old. . . ' 'And when we die
All's over that is ours; and life burns on
Through other lovers, other lips', said I,
'Heart of my heart, our heaven is now, is won!'

'We are Earth's best, that learnt her lesson here.
Life is our cry. We have kept the faith!' we said;
'We shall go down with unreluctant tread
Rose-crowned into the darkness!' . . . Proud we were,
And laughed, that had such brave true things to say.
– And then you suddenly cried, and turned away.

RUPERT BROOKE (1887-1915)

A Charm

Take of English earth as much
As either hand may rightly clutch.
In the taking of it breathe
Prayer for all who lie beneath.
Not the great nor well-bespoke,
But the mere uncounted folk
Of whose life and death is none
Report or lamentation.
Lay that earth upon thy heart,
And thy sickness shall depart!

It shall sweeten and make whole
Fevered breath and festered soul.
It shall mightily restrain
Over-busied hand and brain.
It shall ease thy mortal strife
'Gainst the immortal woe of life,
Till thyself, restored, shall prove
By what grace the Heavens do move.

Take of English flowers these –
Spring's full-facèd primroses,
Summer's wild wide-hearted rose,
Autumn's wall-flower of the close,
And, thy darkness to illume,
Winter's bee-thronged ivy bloom,
Seek and serve them where they bide
From Candlemas to Christmas-tide,
For these simples, used aright,
Can restore a failing sight.

These shall cleanse and purify
Webbed and inward-turning eye;
These shall show thee treasure hid,
Thy familiar fields amid;
And reveal (which is thy need)
Every man a King indeed!

RUDYARD KIPLING (1865-1936)

Leaves

Leaves of the summer, lovely summer's pride,
Sweet is the shade below your lofty tree,
Whether in waving copses, where ye hide
My roamings, or in fields that let me see
The open sky; and whether ye may be
Around the low-stemm'd oak, outspreading wide;
Or taper ash upon the mountain side;
Or lowland elm; your shade is sweet to me.

Whether ye wave above the early flow'rs
In lively green; or whether, rustling sere,
Ye fly on playful winds, around my feet,

In dying autumn; lovely are your bow'rs,
Ye early-dying children of the year;
Holy the silence of your calm retreat.

WILLIAM BARNES (1801-86)

You Love the Roses

You love the roses – so do I. I wish
The sky would rain down roses, as they rain
From off the shaken bush. Why will it not?
Then all the valley would be pink and white
And soft to tread on. They would fall as light
As feathers, smelling sweet: and it would be
Like sleeping and yet waking, all at once.

GEORGE ELIOT (1819-80)

The Fairy Tale

How obstinate the morning is.
Its mist-and-castle fairy tale
Carries us back to nurseries
Where Good must win and Evil fail,
The magic milking-pail

Of days that never could run dry,
Of hopes no disillusion shook,
When only giants had to die,
Heroes immortal, as the book
Shut on a loving look.

Most otherwise the world has proved.
The mists blow off, the castles fade.
The need to love and to be loved
We have a thousand times betrayed,
Ashamed in our own shade.

As rivers sidle to the sea
We rise and wrinkle to our end,
Between the banks of what-must-be
Confined at every reach and bend,
Gradually we descend.

Yet still on mornings such as these
The mirage shifts our channelled course;
Streams run uphill above the trees;
The hero on the enchanted horse
Opens incredible doors.

ROBERT GITTINGS (b 1911)

'Shall I compare thee to a summer's day? . . .'

Shall I compare thee to a summer's day?
Thou art more lovely and more temperate:
Rough winds do shake the darling buds of May,
And summer's lease hath all too short a date:
Sometimes too hot the eye of heaven shines
And often is his gold complexion dimmed;
And every fair from fair sometime declines,
By chance or nature's changing course untrimmed;
But thy eternal summer shall not fade
Nor lose possession of that fair thou owest;
Nor shall Death brag thou wanderest in his shade,
When in eternal lines to time thou growest:
So long as men can breathe or eyes can see,
So long lives this and this gives life to thee.

WILLIAM SHAKESPEARE (1564-1616)

Look at the Grass

Look at the grass, sucked by the seed from dust,
Whose blood is the spring rain, whose food the sun,
Whose life the scythe takes ere the sorrels rust,
Whose stalk is chaff before the winter's done.
Even the grass its happy moment has
In May, when glistening buttercups make gold;
The exulting millions of the meadow-grass
Give out a green thanksgiving from the mould.
Even the blade that has not even a blossom
Creates a mind, its joy's persistent soul
Is a warm spirit on the old earth's bosom
When April's fire has dwindled to a coal;
The spirit of the grasses' joy makes fair
The winter fields when even the wind goes bare.

JOHN MASEFIELD (1878-1967)

Summer Afternoon

Far off the rook, tired by the mid-day beam,
Caws lazily this summer afternoon;
The butterflies, with wandering up and down
O'er flower-bright marsh and meadow, wearied seem;
With vacant gaze, lost in a waking dream,
We, listless, on the busy insects pore,
In rapid dance uncertain, darting o'er
The smooth-spread surface of the tepid stream;
The air is slothful, and will scarce convey
Soft sounds of idle waters to the ear;
In brightly-dim obscurity appear
The distant hills which skirt the landscape gay;
While restless fancy owns the unnerving sway
In visions often changed, but nothing clear.

THOMAS DOUBLEDAY (1790-1870)

A Summer's Evening

Clear had the day been from the dawn,
All chequer'd was the sky,
Thin clouds, like scarfs of cobweb lawn,
Veil'd Heaven's most glorious eye.

The winde had no more strength than this,
That leisurely it blew,
To make one leaf the next to kiss
That closely by it grew.

The rills that on the pebbles play'd
Might now be heard at will;
This world the only music made,
Else everything was still.

The flowers like brave embroidered girls,
Look'd as they most desired
To see whose head with orient pearls
Most curiously was tired;

And to itself the subtle air
Such sovreignty assumes,
That it receiv'd too large a share
From Nature's rich perfumes.

MICHAEL DRAYTON (1563-1631)

The Evening Comes

The evening comes, the fields are still.
The tinkle of the thirsty rill,
Unheard all day, ascends again;
Deserted is the half-mown plain,
Silent the swaths! the ringing wain,
The mower's cry, the dog's alarms,
All housed within the sleeping farms!
The business of the day is done,
The last-left haymaker is gone.
And from the thyme upon the height,
And from the elder-blossom white
And pale dog-roses in the hedge,
And from the mint-plant in the sedge,
In puffs of balm the night-air blows
The perfume which the day forgoes.
And on the pure horizon far,
See, pulsing with the first-born star,
The liquid ·sky above the hill!
The evening comes, the fields are still.

MATTHEW ARNOLD (1822-88)

Fair Weather and Foul

Speak nought, move not, but listen, the sky is full of gold,
No ripple on the river, no stir in field or fold,
All gleams but nought doth glisten, but the far-off unseen sea.

Forget days past, heart broken, put all memory by!
No grief on the hill-side, no pity in the sky,
Joy that may not be spoken fills mead and flower and tree.

WILLIAM MORRIS (1834-96)

The Naturalist's Summer-Evening Walk

When day declining sheds a milder gleam,
What time the may-fly haunts the pool or stream;
When the still owl skims round the grassy mead,
What time the timorous hare limps forth to feed;
Then be the time to steal adown the vale,
And listen to the vagrant cuckoo's tale;
To hear the clamorous curlew call his mate,
Or the soft quail his tender pain relate;
To see the swallow sweep the dark'ning plain
Belated, to support her infant train;
To mark the swift in rapid giddy ring
Dash round the steeple, unsubdu'd of wing:
Amusive birds! say where your hid retreat
When the frost rages and the tempests beat;
Whence your return, by such nice instinct led,
When spring, soft season, lifts her bloomy head?
Such baffled searches mock man's prying pride,
The God of Nature is your secret guide!
While deep'ning shades obscure the face of day,
To yonder bench leaf-shelter'd let us stray,
'Till blended objects fail the swimming sight,
And all the fading landscape sinks in night;

To hear the drowsy dor come brushing by
With buzzing wing, or the shrill cricket cry;
To see the feeding bat glance through the wood;
To catch the distant falling of the flood;
While o'er the cliff th' awaken'd churl-owl hung
Through the still gloom protracts his chattering song;
While high in air, and pois'd upon his wings
Unseen the soft enamour'd woodlark sings:
These, Nature's works, the curious mind employ,
Inspire a soothing, melancholy joy:
As fancy warms, a pleasing kind of pain
Steals o'er the cheek, and thrills the creeping vein!
Each rural sight, each sound, each smell, combine;
The tinkling sheep-bell, or the breath of kine;
The new-mown hay that scents the swelling breeze,
Or cottage-chimney smoking through the trees,
The chilling night-dews fall: – away, retire;
For see, the glow-worm lights her amorous fire!
Thus, ere night's veil had half-obscur'd the sky,
Th'impatient damsel hung her lamp on high:
True to the signal, by love's meteor led,
Leander hastened to his Hero's bed.

GILBERT WHITE (1720-93)

Ode on Solitude

Happy the man whose wish and care
A few paternal acres bound,
Content to breathe his native air,
In his own ground.

Whose herds with milk, whose fields with bread,
Whose flocks supply him with attire,
Whose trees in summer yield him shade,
In winter fire.

Blest, who can unconcern'dly find
Hours, days, and years slide soft away,
In health of body, peace of mind,
Quiet by day,

Sound sleep by night; study and ease,
Together mixt; sweet recreation;
And Innocence, which most does please
With meditation.

Thus let me live, unseen, unknown,
Thus unlamented let me die,
Steal from the world, and not a stone
Tell where I lie.

ALEXANDER POPE (1688-1744)

from *August*

Now came fulfillment of the year's desire;
The tall wheat, coloured by the August fire,
Grew heavy-headed, dreading its decay,
And blacker grew the elm-trees day by day.
About the edges of the yellow corn,
And o'er the gardens grown somewhat outworn
The bees went hurrying to fill up their store;
The apple-boughs bent over more and more;
With peach and apricot the garden wall
Was odorous, and the pears began to fall
From off the high tree with each freshening breeze.

WILLIAM MORRIS (1834-96)

To Marygolds

Give way, and be ye ravisht by the Sun,
(And hang the head when as the Act is done)
Spread as He spreads; wax lesse as He do's wane;
And as He struts, close up to Maids again.

ROBERT HERRICK (1591-1674)

Memory

So shuts the marigold her leaves
At the departure of the sun;
So from the honeysuckle sheaves
The bee goes when the day is done;
So sits the turtle when she is but one,
And so all woe, as I since she is gone.

To some few birds kind Nature hath
Made all the summer as one day:
Which once enjoy'd, cold winter's wrath
As night they sleeping pass away.
Those happy creatures are, that know not yet
The pain to be deprived or to forget.

I oft have heard men say there be
Some that with confidence profess
The helpful Art of Memory:
But could they teach Forgetfulness,
I'd learn; and try what further art could do
To make me love her and forget her too.

WILLIAM BROWNE (1591-?1645)

To Autumn

Season of mists and mellow fruitfulness,
Close bosom-friend of the maturing sun;
Conspiring with him how to load and bless
With fruit the vines that round the thatch-eves run;
To bend with apples the moss'd cottage-trees,
And fill all fruit with ripeness to the core;
To swell the gourd, and plump the hazel shells
With a sweet kernel; to set budding more,
And still more, later flowers for the bees,
Until they think warm days will never cease,
For Summer has o'er-brimm'd their clammy cells.

Who hath not seen thee oft amid thy store?
Sometimes whoever seeks abroad may find
Thee sitting careless on a granary floor,
Thy hair soft-lifted by the winnowing wind;
Or on a half-reap'd furrow sound asleep,
Drows'd with the fume of poppies, while thy hook
Spares the next swath and all its twined flowers:
And sometimes like a gleaner thou dost keep
Steady thy laden head across a brook;
Or by a cyder-press, with patient look,
Thou watchest the last oozings hours by hours.

Where are the songs of Spring? Ay, where are they?
Think not of them, thou hast thy music too, –
While barred clouds bloom the soft-dying day,
And touch the stubble-plains with rosy hue;
Then in a wailful choir the small gnats mourn
Among the river sallows, borne aloft
Or sinking as the light wind lives or dies;
And full-grown lambs loud bleat from hilly bourn;
Hedge-crickets sing; and now with treble soft
The red-breast whistles from a garden-croft;
And gathering swallows twitter in the skies.

JOHN KEATS (1795-1821)

The Lane

Some day, I think, there will be people enough
In Froxfield to pick all the blackberries
Out of the hedges of Green Lane, the straight
Broad lane where now September hides herself
In bracken and blackberry, harebell and dwarf gorse.
To-day, where yesterday a hundred sheep
Were nibbling, halcyon bells shake to the sway
Of waters that no vessel ever sailed . . .
It is a kind of spring: the chaffinch tries
His song. For heat it is like summer too.
This might be winter's quiet. While the glint
Of hollies dark in the swollen hedges lasts –
One mile – and those bells ring, little I know
Or heed if time be still the same, until
The lane ends and once more all is the same.

EDWARD THOMAS (1878-1917)

Blackberry Picking

Late August, given heavy rain and sun
For a full week, the blackberries would ripen.
At first, just one, a glossy purple clot
Among others, red, green, hard as a knot.
You ate that first one and its flesh was sweet
Like thickened wine: summer's blood was in it
Leaving stains upon the tongue and lust for
Picking. Then red ones inked up and that hunger
Sent us out with milk-cans, pea-tins, jam-pots
Where briars scratched and wet grass bleached our boots
Round hayfields, cornfields and potato-drills
We trekked and picked until the cans were full,
Until the tinkling bottom had been covered
With green ones, and on top big dark blobs burned
Like a plate of eyes. Our hands were peppered
With thorn pricks, our palms sticky as Bluebeard's.

We hoarded the fresh berries in the byre.
But when the bath was filled we found a fur,
A rat-grey fungus, glutting on our cache.
The juice was stinking too. Once off the bush
The fruit fermented, the sweet flesh would turn sour.
I always felt like crying. It wasn't fair
That all the lovely canfuls smelt of rot.
Each year I hoped they'd keep, knew they would not.

SEAMUS HEANEY (b 1939)

from *The Autumn Robin*

Sweet little bird in russet coat
The livery of the closing year
I love thy lonely plaintive note
And tiney whispering song to hear
While on the stile or garden seat
I sit to watch the falling leaves
Thy songs thy little joys repeat
My loneliness relieves

JOHN CLARE (1793-1864)

An Answer

Come, let us go into the lane, love mine,
And mark and gather what the Autumn grows:
The creamy elder mellowed into wine,
The russet hip that was the pink-white rose;
The amber woodbine into rubies turned,
The blackberry that was the bramble born;
Nor let the seeded clematis be spurned,
Nor pearls, that now are corals, of the thorn,
Look! what a lovely posy we have made
From the wild garden of the waning year.
So when, dear love, your summer is decayed,
Beauty more touching than is clustered here
Will linger in your life, and I shall cling
Closely as now, nor ask if it be Spring.

ALFRED AUSTIN (1835-1913)

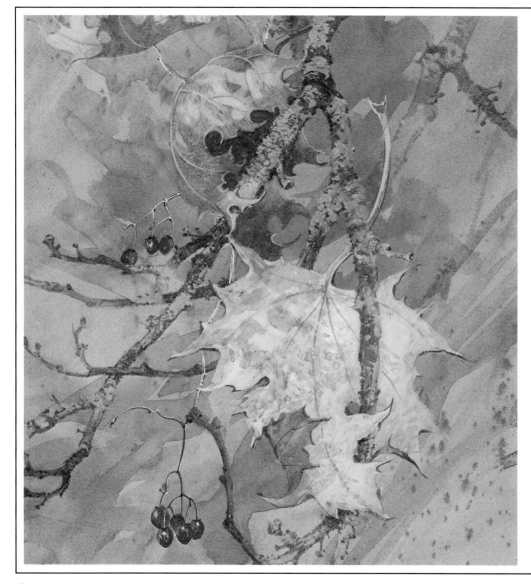

Fall, Leaves

Fall, leaves, fall; die, flowers, away;
Lengthen night and shorten day:
Every leaf speaks bliss to me,
Fluttering from the autumn tree;

I shall smile when wreaths of snow
Blossom where the rose should grow:
I shall sing when night's decay
Ushers in the drearier day.

EMILY BRONTË (1818-48)

Falling Leaves

Whirled dust, world dust,
Tossed and torn from trees,
No more they labour for life, no more
Shelter of green glade, shade
Of apples under leaf, lifted in air
They soar, no longer leaves.

What, wind that bears me,
Am I about to be? Will water
Draw me down among its multitude?
Earth shall I return, shall I return to the tree?
Or by fire go further
From myself than now I can know or dare?

KATHLEEN RAINE (b 1908)

Autumnal

Pale amber sunlight falls across
The reddening October trees,
That hardly sway before a breeze
As soft as summer: summer's loss
Seems little, dear! on days like these

Let misty autumn be our part!
The twilight of the year is sweet:
Where shadow and the darkness meet
Our love, a twilight of the heart
Eludes a little time's deceit.

Are we not better and at home
In dreamful Autumn, we who deem
No harvest joy is worth a dream?
A little while and night shall come,
A little while, then, let us dream.

Beyond the pearled horizons lie
Winter and night: awaiting these
We garner this poor hour of ease,
Until love turn from us and die
Beneath the drear November trees.

ERNEST DOWSON (1867-1900)

Late Leaves

The leaves are falling; so am I;
The few late flowers have moisture in the eye;
So have I too.
Scarcely on any bough is heard
Joyous, or even unjoyous bird
The whole wood through.

Winter may come: he brings but nigher
His circle (yearly narrowing) to the fire
Where old friends meet.
Let him; now heaven is overcast,
And spring and summer both are past,
And all things sweet.

WALTER SAVAGE LANDOR (1775-1864)

Autumn: A Dirge

The warm sun is failing, the bleak wind is wailing,
The bare boughs are sighing, the pale flowers are dying,
And the year
On the earth her deathbed, in a shroud of leaves dead,
Is lying.
Come, months, come away,
From November to May,
In your saddest array;
Follow the bier
Of the dead cold year,
And like dim shadows watch by her sepulchre.

The chill rain is falling, the nipt worm is crawling,
The rivers are swelling, the thunder is knelling
For the year;
The blithe swallows are flown, and the lizards each gone
To his dwelling;
Come on white, black, and grey,
Let your light sisters play —
Ye, follow the bier
Of the dead cold year,
And make her grave green with tear on tear.

PERCY BYSSHE SHELLEY (1792-1822)

To the Owl

Sad bird of night, what sorrows call thee forth,
To vent thy plaints thus in the midnight hour?
Is it some blast that gathers in the north,
Threatening to nip the verdure of thy bower?

Is it, sad owl, that Autumn strips the shade,
And leaves thee here, unsheltered and forlorn?
Or fear that Winter will thy nest invade?
Or friendless melancholy bids thee mourn?

Shut out, lone bird, from all the feathered train,
To tell thy sorrows to the unheeding gloom;
No friend to pity when thou dost complain,
Grief all thy thought, and solitude thy home.

Sing on, sad mourner! I will bless thy strain,
And pleased in sorrow listen to thy song;
Sing on, sad mourner! to the night complain,
While the lone echo wafts thy notes along.

Is beauty less when down the glowing cheek
Sad, piteous tears in native sorrows fall?
Less kind the heart when anguish bids it break?
Less happy he who lists to pity's call?

Ah no, sad owl! nor is thy voice less sweet
That sadness tunes it, and that grief is there;
That Spring's gay notes, unskilled, thou canst repeat;
That sorrow bids thee to the gloom repair.

Nor that the treble songsters of the day
Are quite estranged, sad bird of night, from thee;
Nor that the thrush deserts the evening spray
When darkness calls thee from thy reverie –

From some old tower, thy melancholy dome,
While the gray walls and desert solitudes
Return each note, responsive to the gloom
Of ivied coverts and surrounding woods.

There hooting, I will list more pleased to thee
Than ever lover to the nightingale;
Or drooping wretch, oppressed with misery,
Lending his ear to some condoling tale.

ROBERT BURNS (1759-96)

The Question

I dreamed that, as I wandered by the way,
Bare winter suddenly was changed to spring
And gentle odours led my steps astray,
Mixed with a sound of waters murmuring
Along a shelving bank of turf, which lay
Under a copse, and hardly dared to fling
Its green arms round the bosom of the stream,
But kissed it and then fled, as thou mightest in dream.

There grew pied wind-flowers and violets,
Daisies, those pearled Arcturi of the earth,
The constellated flower that never sets;
Faint oxlips; tender bluebells, at whose birth
The sod scarce heaved; and that tall flower that wets
Its mother's face with heaven-collected tears,
When the low wind, its playmate's voice, it hears.

And in the warm hedge grew lush eglantine,
Green cowbind and the moonlight-coloured May,
And cherry blossoms, and white cups, whose wine
Was the bright dew yet drained not by the day;
And wild roses, and ivy serpentine,
With its dark buds and leaves, wandering astray;
And flowers azure, black and streaked with gold,
Fairer than any wakened eyes behold.

And nearer to the river's trembling edge
There grew broad flag flowers, purple prankt with white.
And starry river buds among the sedge,
And floating water-lilies, broad and bright,
Which lit the oak that overhung the hedge
With moonlight beams of their own watery light;
And bulrushes, and reeds of such deep green
As soothed the dazzled eye with sober sheen.

Methought that of these visionary flowers
I made a nosegay, bound in such a way
That the same hues, which in their natural bowers
Were mingled or opposed, the like array
Kept these imprisoned children of the Hours
Within my hand, - and then, elate and gay.
I hastened to the spot whence I had come,
That I might there present it! - Oh! to whom?

PERCY BYSSHE SHELLEY (1792-1822)

from *Winter*

With the fierce rage of Winter deep suffus'd,
An icy gale, oft shifting, o'er the pool
Breathes a blue film, and in its mid career
Arrests the bickering stream. The loosen'd ice,
Let down the flood, and half dissolv'd by day,
Rustles no more; but to the sedgy bank
Fast grows, or gathers round the pointed stone,
A crystal pavement, by the breath of heaven
Cemented firm; till, seiz'd from shore to shore,
The whole imprison'd river growls below.
Loud rings the frozen earth, and hard reflects
A double noise; while, at his evening watch,
The village dog deters the nightly thief;
The heifer lows; the distant water-fall
Swells in the breeze; and, with the hasty tread
Of traveller, the hollow-sounding plain
Shakes from afar. The full ethereal round,
Infinite worlds disclosing to the view,
Shines out intensely keen; and, all one cope
Of starry glitter glows from pole to pole.

From pole to pole, the rigid influence falls,
Thro the still night, incessant, heavy, strong,
And seizes Nature fast. It freezes on;
Till morn, late-rising o'er the drooping world,
Lifts her pale eye unjoyous. Then appears
The various labour of the silent night:
Prone from the dripping eave, and dumb cascade,
Whose idle torrents only seem to roar,
The pendant icicle; the frost-work fair,
Where transient hues and fancy'd figures rise;
Wide-spouted o'er the hill the frozen brook,
A livid tract, cold-gleaming on the morn;
The forest bent beneath the plumy wave;
And by the frost refin'd the whiter snow,
Incrusted hard, and sounding to the tread
Of early shepherd, as he pensive seeks
His pining flock, or from the mountain-top,
Pleas'd with the slippery surface, swift descends.

JAMES THOMSON (1700-48)

Winter

In rigorous hours, when down the iron lane
The redbreast looks in vain
For hips and haws,
Lo, shining flowers upon my window-pane
The silver pencil of the winter draws.

When all the snowy hill
And the bare woods are still;
When snipes are silent in the frozen bogs,
And all the garden garth is whelmed in mire,
Lo, by the hearth, the laughter of the logs –
More fair than roses, lo, the flowers of fire!

ROBERT LOUIS STEVENSON (1850-94)

Winter

Old January clad in crispy rime
Comes hirpling on and often makes a stand
The hasty snowstorm neer disturbs his time
He mends no pace but beats his dithering hand
And February like a timid maid
Smiling and sorrowing follows in his train
Huddled in cloak of mirey roads affraid
She hastens on to greet her home again
Then March the prophetess by storms inspired
Gazes in rapture on the troubled sky
And then in headlong fury madly fired
She bids the hail storm boil and hurry bye
Yet neath the blackest cloud a sunbeam flings
Its cheering promise of returning spring.

JOHN CLARE (1793-1864)

Winter

The merciful sweet influence of the South
Cheereth the hardy winter-buds no more;
No scented breath hovers around their mouth,
No beauty in their bosoms to adore!
With icy foot the rude North treads them down,
And tells them they shall never greet the Spring,
But perish at the line of Winter's frown,
That kills the very hope of blossoming!
Thus while he fans them with his frosty wing
They scatter all their leaves upon the earth, –
Not worth the hapless ruddock's gathering, –
And die upon the spot that gave them birth!
How like in fate the winter-bud and I,
We live in sorrow, and in sorrow die!

GEORGE DARLEY (1795-1846)

Thaw

Over the land freckled with snow half-thawed
The speculating rooks at their nests cawed
And saw from elm-tops, delicate as flower of grass,
What we below could not see, Winter pass.

EDWARD THOMAS (1878-1917)

from *February*

The change has come at last, and from the west
Drives on the wind, and gives the clouds no rest,
And ruffles up the water thin that lies
Over the surface of the thawing ice;
Sunrise and sunset with no glorious show
Are seen, as late they were across the snow;
The wet-lipped west wind chilleth to the bone
More than the light and flickering east hath done.
Full soberly the earth's fresh hope begins,
Nor stays to think of what each new day wins:
And still it seems to bid us turn away
From this chill thaw to dream of blossomed May . . .

WILLIAM MORRIS (1834-96)

Life of Last Year

Though now, while the March wind is keen,
The holly and ivy are green,
We ev'rywhere see in our walks,
By hedge or by wood, wither'd stalks;
Some stout that, unholden, have stood;
Some weak that have hung on green wood,
But beaten by rain, and by hail,
And snow, in the winterly gale,
Now totter or quiver all sear,
Dead shapes of the life of last year.

The teazle, although with a head
Spike-warded, is now smitten dead;
And nettles, with spears threat'ning pain
Of poison, are yet winter-slain.
All dry are the cow-parsley shoots,
And hemlock is pale to the roots.
The bryony's rotted away,
And clivers lose hold of the spray.
And all are now bloomless and sear,
Dead shapes of the life of last year.

But still, of the wort-life that sprung
When last summer's birdlings were young,
Good shapes, from the ground and the bough,
Are lingering on with us now.
Or apples or nuts from the trees,
Long beans or white ballkins of peas,
Or if thistledown fly on the wind,
Our own and our little ones' meat,
And may it be never too dear
For old and for young through the year.

WILLIAM BARNES (1801-86)

Snow Drop

The blanched melted snows
Fill the plant's stem, a capillary
Of heightened moisture. Air weights
Round a white head hanging
Above granuled earth.
There, are three scarab-like petals,
Open, an insect's carapace
With a creature in these, poised.

It does not move. A white
Cylinder with two
Thin bands of green, broken
Away where that part finishes.
There is no more.
The sun's heat reaches the flower
Of the snowdrop.

JON SILKIN (b 1930)

The Lamb

Little Lamb, who made thee?
Dost thou know who made thee?
Gave thee life, and bid thee feed,
By the stream and o'er the mead;
Gave thee clothing of delight,
Softest clothing, woolly, bright;
Gave thee such a tender voice,
Making all the vales rejoice?
Little Lamb, who made thee?
Dost thou know who made thee?

Little Lamb, I'll tell thee,
Little Lamb, I'll tell thee:
He is calléd by thy name,
For He calls Himself a Lamb.
He is meek, and He is mild;
He became a little child.
I a child, and thou a lamb,
We are calléd by His name.
Little Lamb, God bless thee!
Little Lamb, God bless thee!

WILLIAM BLAKE (1757-1827)

All Nature Has a Feeling

All nature has a feeling: woods, fields, brooks
Are life eternal – and in silence they
Speak happiness – beyond the reach of books.
There's nothing mortal in them – their decay
Is the green life of change, to pass away
And come again in blooms revivified.
Its birth was heaven, eternal is its stay,
And with the sun and moon shall still abide
Beneath their night and day and heaven wide.

JOHN CLARE (1793-1864)

A Backward Spring

The trees are afraid to put forth buds,
And there is timidity in the grass:
The plots lie gray where gouged by spuds,
And whether next week will pass
Free of sly sour winds is the fret of each bush
Of barberry waiting to bloom.

Yet the snowdrop's face betrays no gloom,
And the primrose pants in its heedless push,
Though the myrtle asks if it's worth the fight
This year with frost and rime
To venture one more time
On delicate leaves and buttons of white
From the selfsame bough as at last year's prime,
And never to ruminate on or remember
What happened to it in mid-December.

THOMAS HARDY (1840-1928)

A Lesson

There is a flower, the Lesser Celandine,
That shrinks like many more from cold and rain,
And the first moment that the sun may shine,
Bright as the sun himself, 'tis out again!

While hailstones have been falling, swarm on swarm,
Or blasts the green field and the trees distrest,
Oft have I seen it muffled up from harm
In close self-shelter, like a thing at rest.

But lately, one rough day, this flower I past,
And recognized it, though an alter'd form,
Now standing forth an offering to the blast,
And buffeted at will by rain and storm.

I stopp'd and said, with inly-mutter'd voice,
'It doth not love the shower, nor seek the cold;
This neither is its courage nor its choice,
But its necessity in being old.

'The sunshine may not cheer it, nor the dew;
It cannot help itself in its decay;
Stiff in its members, wither'd, changed of hue,' –
And, in my spleen, I smiled that it was gray.

To be a prodigal's favourite – then, worse truth,
A miser's pensioner – behold our lot!
O Man! that from thy fair and shining youth
Age might but take the things Youth needed not!

WILLIAM WORDSWORTH (1770-1850)

The Primrose

Ask me why I send you here
This sweet Infanta of the year?
Ask me why I send to you
This primrose, thus bepearl'd with dew?
I will whisper to your ears:-
The sweets of love are mix'd with tears.

Ask me why this flower does show
So yellow-green, and sickly too?
Ask me why the stalk is weak
And bending (yet it doth not break)?
I will answer:- These discover
What fainting hopes are in a lover.

ROBERT HERRICK (1591-1674)

The Primrose

Dost ask me, why I send thee here,
This firstling of the infant year –
This lovely native of the vale,
That hangs so pensive and so pale?

Look on its bending stalk, so weak
That, each way yielding, doth not break,
And see how aptly it reveals
The doubts and fears a lover feels.

Look on its leaves of yellow hue
Bepearl'd thus with morning dew,
And these will whisper in thine ears
'The sweets of love are wash'd with tears.'

ROBERT BURNS (1759-96)

The Hills

Out of the complicated house, come I
To walk beneath the sky.
Here mud and stones and turf, here everything
Is mutely comforting.
Now hung upon the twigs and thorns appear
A host of lovely rain-drops cold and clear.
And on the bank
Or deep in brambly hedges dank
The small birds nip about, and say:
"Brothers, the Spring is not so far away!"
The hills like mother-giantesses old
Lie in the cold.
And with a complete patience, let
The cows come cropping on their bosoms wet,
And even tolerate that such as I
Should wander by
With paltry leathern heel which cannot harm
Their bodies calm;
And, with a heart they cannot know, to bless
The enormous power of their peacefulness.

FRANCES CORNFORD (1886-1960)

The Mid-Day Verse

The Sun has climbed the hill, the day is on the downward slope,
Between the morning and the afternoon, stand I here with
   my soul, and lift it up.
My soul is heavy with sunshine, and steeped with strength.
The sunbeams have filled me like a honeycomb,
It is the moment of fulness,
And the top of the morning.

D.H. LAWRENCE (1885-1930)

To the Skylark

Ethereal minstrel! pilgrim of the sky!
Dost thou despise the earth where cares abound?
Or while the wings aspire, are heart and eye
Both with thy nest upon the dewy ground?
Thy nest which thou canst drop into at will,
Those quivering wings composed, that music still!

To the last point of vision, and beyond
Mount, daring warbler! – that love-prompted strain
– 'Twixt thee and thine a never-failing bond –
Thrills not the less the bosom of the plain:
Yet might'st thou seem, proud privilege! to sing
All independent of the leafy Spring.

Leave to the nightingale her shady wood;
A privacy of glorious light is thine,
Whence thou dost pour upon the world a flood
Of harmony, with instinct more divine;
Type of the wise, who soar, but never roam –
True to the kindred points of Heaven and Home.

WILLIAM WORDSWORTH (1770-1850)

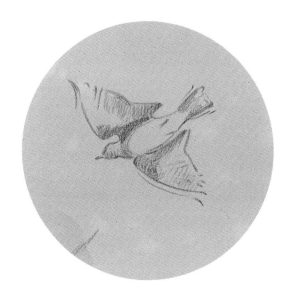

The Daffodils

I wander'd lonely as a cloud
That floats on high o'er vales and hills,
When all at once I saw a crowd,
A host of golden daffodils,
Beside the lake, beneath the trees
Fluttering and dancing in the breeze.

Continuous as the stars that shine
And twinkle on the milky way,
They stretched in never-ending line
Along the margin of a bay;
Ten thousand saw I at a glance
Tossing their heads in sprightly dance.

The waves beside them danced, but they
Out-did the sparkling waves in glee:-
A Poet could not but be gay
In such a jocund company!
I gazed – and gazed – but little thought
What wealth the show to me had brought;

For oft, when on my couch I lie
In vacant or in pensive mood,
They flash upon that inward eye
Which is the bliss of solitude;
And then my heart with pleasure fills,
And dances with the daffodils.

WILLIAM WORDSWORTH (1770-1850)

The Spring

Now that the winter's gone, the earth hath lost
Her snow-white robes; and now no more the frost
Candies the grasse, or castes an ycie creame
Upon the silver Lake or Chrystall streame:
But the warme Sunne thawes the benummed earth,
And makes it tender; gives a sacred birth
To the dead Swallow; wakes in hollow tree
The drowzie Cuckow and the Humble-Bee.
Now doe a quire of chirping minstrels bring,
In tryumph to the world, the youthfull Spring.
The vallies, hills, and woods in rich araye
Welcome the comming of the long'd-for May.

THOMAS CAREW (?1595-?1640)

Home

Often I had gone this way before:
But now it seemed I never could be
And never had been anywhere else;
'Twas home; one nationality
We had, I and the birds that sang,
One memory.

They welcomed me. I had come back
That eve somehow from somewhere far:
The April mist, the chill, the calm,
Meant the same thing familiar
And pleasant to us, and strange too,
Yet with no bar.

The thrush on the oaktop in the lane
Sang his last song, or last but one;
And as he ended, on the elm
Another had but just begun
His last; they knew no more than I
The day was done.

Then past his dark white cottage front
A labourer went along, his tread
Slow, half with weariness, half with ease;
And, through the silence, from his shed
The sound of sawing rounded all
That silence said.

EDWARD THOMAS (1878-1917)

Matin Song

Pack, clouds, away! and welcome, day!
With night we banish sorrow.
Sweet air, blow soft; mount, lark, aloft
To give my Love good-morrow!
Wings from the wind to please her mind,
Notes from the lark I'll borrow:
Bird, prune thy wing! nightingale, sing!
To give my Love good-morrow!
To give my Love good-morrow
Notes from them all I'll borrow.

Wake from thy nest, robin red-breast!
Sing, birds, in every furrow!
And from each bill let music shrill
Give my fair Love good-morrow!
Blackbird and thrush in every bush,
Stare, linnet, and cocksparrow,
You pretty elves, among yourselves
Sing my fair Love good-morrow!
To give my Love good-morrow!
Sing, birds, in every furrow!

THOMAS HEYWOOD (157?-1650)

Aubade

Hark, hark! the lark at heaven's gate sings,
And Phoebus 'gins arise,
His steeds to water at those springs
On chalic'd flow'rs that lies;
And winking Mary-buds begin
To ope their golden eyes.
With everything that pretty bin,
My lady sweet, arise;
Arise, arise!

WILLIAM SHAKESPEARE (1564-1616)

Pippa's Song

The year's at the spring,
And day's at the morn;
Morning's at seven;
The hill-side's dew-pearl'd;
The lark's on the wing;
The snail's on the thorn;
God's in His heaven –
All's right with the world!

ROBERT BROWNING (1812-89)

A Chanted Calendar

First came the primrose,
On the bank high,
Like a maiden looking forth
From the window of a tower
When the battle rolls below,
So look'd she,
And saw the storms go by.

Then came the wind-flower
In the valley left behind,
As a wounded maiden, pale
With purple streaks of woe,
When the battle has roll'd by
Wanders to and fro,
So totter'd she,
Dishevell'd in the wind.

Then came the daisies,
On the first of May,
Like a banner'd show's advance
While the crowd runs by the way,
With ten thousand flowers about them
 they came trooping through the fields.
As a happy people come,
So came they,
As a happy people come
When the war has roll'd away,
With dance and tabor, pipe and drum,
And all make holiday.

Then came the cowslip,
Like a dancer in the fair,
She spread her little mat of green,
And on it danced she.
With a fillet bound about her brow,
A fillet round her happy brow,
A golden fillet round her brow,
And rubies in her hair.

SYDNEY DOBELL (1824-74)

To the Cuckoo

Hail, beauteous stranger of the grove!
Thou messenger of Spring!
Now Heaven repairs thy rural seat,
And woods thy welcome ring.

What time the daisy decks the green,
Thy certain voice we hear:
Hast thou a star to guide thy path,
Or mark the rolling year?

Delightful visitant! with thee
I hail the time of flowers,
And hear the sound of music sweet
From birds among the bowers.

The schoolboy, wand'ring through the wood
To pull the primrose gay,
Starts, the new voice of Spring to hear,
And imitates thy lay.

JOHN LOGAN (1748-88)

To the Cuckoo

O blithe new-comer! I have heard,
I hear thee and rejoice:
O Cuckoo! shall I call thee bird,
Or but a wandering Voice?

While I am lying on the grass
Thy twofold shout I hear;
From hill to hill it seems to pass,
At once far off and near.

Though babbling only to the vale
Of sunshine and of flowers,
Thou bringest unto me a tale
Of visionary hours.

Thrice welcome, darling of the Spring!
Even yet thou art to me
No bird, but an invisible thing,
A voice, a mystery;

The same whom in my school-boy days
I listen'd to; that Cry
Which made me look a thousand ways
In bush, and tree, and sky.

To seek thee did I often rove
Through woods and on the green;
And thou wert still a hope, a love;
Still long'd for, never seen!

And I can listen to thee yet;
Can lie upon the plain
And listen, till I do beget
That golden time again.

O blessèd Bird! the earth we pace
Again appears to be
An unsubstantial, fairy place,
That is fit home for Thee!

WILLIAM WORDSWORTH (1770-1850)

Loveliest of Trees

Loveliest of trees, the cherry now
Is hung with bloom along the bough,
And stands about the woodland ride
Wearing white for Eastertide.

Now, of my threescore years and ten,
Twenty will not come again,
And take from seventy springs a score,
It only leaves me fifty more.

And since to look at things in bloom
Fifty springs are little room,
About the woodlands I will go
To see the cherry hung with snow.

A.E. HOUSMAN (1859-1936)

To Blossoms

Fair pledges of a fruitful tree,
Why do ye fall so fast?
Your date is not so past
But you may stay yet here awhile
To blush and gently smile,
And go at last.

What! were ye born to be
An hour or half's delight,
And so to bid good night?
'Twas pity Nature brought you forth
Merely to show your worth
And lose you quite.

But you are lovely leaves, where we
May read how soon things have
Their end, though ne'er so brave:
And after they have shown their pride
Like you awhile, they glide
Into the grave.

ROBERT HERRICK (1591-1674)

Pied Beauty

Glory be to God for dappled things –
For skies of couple-colour as a brinded cow;
For rose-moles all in stipple upon trout that swim;
Fresh-firecoal chestnut-falls; finches' wings;
Landscape plotted and pieced – fold, fallow, and plough;
And all trades, their gear and tackle and trim.

All things counter, original, spare, strange;
Whatever is fickle, freckled (who knows how?)
With swift, slow; sweet, sour; adazzle, dim;
He fathers-forth whose beauty is past change:
Praise him.

GERARD MANLEY HOPKINS (1844-89)

The Linnet

I heard a linnet courting
His lady in the spring:
His mates were idly sporting,
Nor stayed to hear him sing
His song of love. –
I fear my speech distorting
His tender love.

The phrases of his pleading
Were full of young delight;
And she that gave him heeding
Interpreted aright
His gay, sweet notes, –
So sadly marred in the reading, –
His tender notes.

And when he ceased, the hearer
Awaited the refrain,
Till swiftly perching nearer
He sang his song again,
His pretty song: –
Would that my verse spake clearer
His tender song!

Ye happy, airy creatures!
That in the merry spring
Think not of what misfeatures
Or cares the year may bring;
But unto love
Resign your simple natures
To tender love.

ROBERT BRIDGES (1844-1930)

Deer

Shy in their herding dwell the fallow deer.
They are spirits of wild sense. Nobody near
Comes upon their pastures. There a life they live,
Of sufficient beauty, phantom, fugitive,
Treading as in jungles free leopards do,
Printless as eyelight, instant as dew.
The great kine are patient, and home-coming sheep
Know our bidding. The fallow deer keep
Delicate and far their counsels wild,
Never to be folded reconciled
To the spoiling hand as the poor flocks are;
Lightfoot, and swift, and unfamiliar,
These you may not hinder, unconfined
Beautiful flocks of the mind.

JOHN DRINKWATER (1882-1937)

The Enkindled Spring

This spring as it comes bursts up in bonfires green,
Wild puffing of green fire trees, and flame green bushes,
Thorn-blossom lifting in wreaths of smoke between
Where the wood fumes up, and the flickering, watery rushes.

I am amazed at this Spring, this conflagration
Of green fires lit on the soil of earth, this blaze
Of growing, these smoke-puffs that puff in wild gyration,
Faces of people blowing across my gaze!

And I, what sort of fire am I among
This conflagration of Spring? the gap in it all - !
Not even palish smoke like the rest of the throng.
Less then the wind that runs to the flamy call!

D.H. LAWRENCE (1885-1930)

Vegetation

O never harm the dreaming world,
the world of green, the world of leaves,
but let its million palms unfold
the adoration of the trees.

It is a love in darkness wrought
obedient to the unseen sun,
longer than memory, a thought
deeper than the graves of time.

The turning spindles of the cells
weave a slow forest over space,
the dance of love, creation,
out of time moves not a leaf,
and out of summer, not a shade.

KATHLEEN RAINE (b 1908)

The Way Through the Woods

They shut the road through the woods
Seventy years ago.
Weather and rain have undone it again,
And now you would never know
There was once a road through the woods
Before they planted the trees.
It is underneath the coppice and heath,
And the thin anemones.
Only the keeper sees
That, where the ring-dove broods,
And the badgers roll at ease,
There was once a road through the woods.

Yet, if you enter the woods
Of a summer evening late,
When the night-air cools on the trout-ringed pools
Where the otter whistles his mate.
They fear not men in the woods,
Because they see so few
You will hear the beat of a horse's feet,
And the swish of a skirt in the dew,
Steadily cantering through
The misty solitudes,
As though they perfectly knew
The old lost road through the woods.
But there is no road through the woods.

RUDYARD KIPLING (1865-1936)

from *The Deserted Village*

Sweet smiling village, loveliest of the lawn,
Thy sports are fled and all thy charms withdrawn;
Amidst thy bowers the tyrant's hand is seen,
And desolation saddens all thy green:
One only master grasps the whole domain,
And half a tillage stints thy smiling plain:
No more thy glassy brook reflects the day,
But, choked with sedges, works its weedy way.
Along thy glades, a solitary guest,
The hollow-sounding bittern guards its nest;
Amidst thy desert walks the lapwing flies,
And tires their echoes with unvaried cries.
Sunk are thy bowers in shapeless ruin all,
And the long grass o'ertops the mouldering wall;
And trembling, shrinking from the spoiler's hand,
Far, far away, thy children leave the land.

Ill fares the land, to hastening ills a prey,
Where wealth accumulates and men decay:
Princes and lords may flourish or may fade;
A breath can make them, as a breath has made;
But a bold peasantry, their country's pride,
When once destroyed, can never be supplied.

A time there was, ere England's griefs began,
When every rood of ground maintained its man;
For him light labour spread her wholesome store,
Just gave what life required, but gave no more:
His best companions, innocence and health;
And his best riches, ignorance of wealth.

But times are altered; trade's unfeeling train
Usurp the land and dispossess the swain;
Along the lawn, where scattered hamlets rose,
Unwieldy wealth and cumbrous pomp repose;
And every want to opulence allied,
And every pang that folly pays to pride.
These gentle hours that plenty bade to bloom,
Those calm desires that asked but litle room,
Those healthful sports that graced the peaceful scene,
Lived in each look and brightened all the green;
These, far departing, seek a kinder shore,
And rural mirth and manners are no more.

OLIVER GOLDSMITH (1728-74)

Harvest Hymn

We spray the fields and scatter
The poison on the ground
So that no wicked wild flowers
Upon our farm be found.
We like whatever helps us
To line our purse with pence;
The twenty-four-hour broiler-house
And neat electric fence.

All concrete sheds around us
And Jaguars in the yard,
The telly lounge and deep-freeze
Are ours from working hard.

We fire the fields for harvest,
The hedges swell the flame,
The oak trees and the cottages
From which our fathers came.
We give no compensation,
The earth is ours today,
And if we lose on arable,
Then bungalows will pay.

All concrete sheds . . . etc.

JOHN BETJEMAN (1906-84)

The Future of Forestry

How will the legend of the age of trees
Feel, when the last tree falls in England?
When the concrete spreads and the town conquers
The country's heart; when contraceptive
Tarmac's laid where farm has faded,
Tramline flows where slept a hamlet,
And shop-fronts, blazing without a stop from
Dover to Wrath, have glazed us over?
Simplest tales will then bewilder
The questioning children, 'What was a chestnut?
Say what it means to climb a Beanstalk.
Tell me, grandfather, what an elm is.
What was Autumn? They never taught us.'
Then, told by teachers how once from mould
Came growing creatures of lower nature
Able to live and die, though neither
Beast nor man, and around them wreathing
Excellent clothing, breathing sunlight –
Half understanding, their ill-acquainted
Fancy will tint their wonder-paintings
– Trees as men walking, wood-romances
Of goblins stalking in silky green,
Of milk-sheen froth upon the lace of hawthorn's
Collar, pallor on the face of birchgirl.
So shall a homeless time, though dimly
Catch from afar (for soul is watchful)
A sight of tree-delighted Eden.

C.S. LEWIS (1898-1963)